First Facts®

ALL ABOUT MEDIA

WHAT IS MEDIA?

BRIEN J JENNINGS

raintree
a Capstone company — publishers for children

Raintree is an imprint of Capstone Global Library Limited, a company incorporated in England and Wales having its registered office at 264 Banbury Road, Oxford, OX2 7DY – Registered company number: 6695582

www.raintree.co.uk
myorders@raintree.co.uk

ISBN 978 1 4747 5440 8
22 21 20 19 18
10 9 8 7 6 5 4 3 2 1

Editorial credits:
Erika L. Shores, editor; Juliette Peters, designer;
Morgan Walters, media researcher; Kathy McColley, production specialist
Printed and bound in India

Photo credits:
Capstone Studio: Karon Dubke, 5; Shutterstock: advent, 20, Andrey_Popov, 19, Artur. B, design element, Chaiwut, 9, Everett Collection, 14, Iakov Filimonov, 11, lenisecalleja.photography, 15, Maxx-Studio, 17, MNStudio, Cover, mongione, 4, patat, 13, Supphachai Salaeman, design element throughout, TonyV3112, 8, Twin Design, 21, vectorfusionart, 7

British Library Cataloguing in Publication Data
A full catalogue record for this book is available from the British Library.

Contents

Media, media everywhere!

Media is talked about all the time because it's everywhere. Look around and you'll see many examples. Media might be something we hear, see or even wear on our clothes. Books, TV programmes, news reports, the internet and video games are also types of media.

Look!

Look at your clothes. Can you see a **logo** anywhere? Logos are an example of media.

What is media literacy?

Media literacy means understanding books, TV programmes, stories, music and their messages. We understand who made the media and why. People write messages for an **audience**. The audience is anyone who may see the media.

logo symbol of a company's brand
audience people who hear, read or see a message

5

Getting to know media

The word media can mean a lot of things. Media refers to the tools we use to share messages, ideas and information with other people. There are many types of media. The main types are print, **recorded** and **broadcast**.

We use media in different ways. Sometimes we listen, watch or read. Sometimes we do all three at the same time, such as watching a football match on TV.

Media is used for three main reasons:
1. To inform or educate
2. To entertain
3. To persuade, which means to make you believe something is true

---

recorded written or filmed so that it can be used or seen again in the future

broadcast TV or radio programme

Print media

Print is the oldest type of media. Words or pictures are written on paper, cloth or another surface. Print media includes newspapers, magazines and books. **Billboards**, posters and even a T-shirt with a logo are print media too.

billboard large outdoor sign used to advertise products or services

Recordings: sound and films

Recordings are sounds or images that are stored. The recordings can be listened to and watched at a later time. When you listen to music or watch a film, it is most likely a recording.

The first sound recordings were made in the 1800s. They were made using paper, foil or wax. The only way to listen to these recordings was to use a phonograph. This machine had to be cranked by hand, and the sound **quality** wasn't very good.

quality standard of
    something as measured
    against other things of
    a similar type

The first film was made in 1878. Today it wouldn't seem like much of a film at all. It didn't tell a story or have people in it. It was just a horse running. Early films were also silent. The first film with sound came out in 1927.

Over time people came up with new ways to record sound and pictures. People today can listen to music and watch films almost anywhere using mobile phones, laptops and tablets.

Think about it!

How do you listen to music?
Where are some of the places
you watch films or videos?

Broadcast media

Do you enjoy listening to the radio or watching TV? If so, then you are using broadcast media. This type of media uses radio waves to carry sound and images.

The radio became popular in the 1920s. Most people listened to the radio for news and entertainment until TV took over in the 1950s. TV quickly became a popular source for news and information.

Advertising and the media

Advertisements are common in a lot of types of media. Advertisements on radio and TV try to get people to buy products and services. Large billboards show photos of famous people or logos. Posters show the latest films coming to cinemas. Can you think of other ways advertisements are used in different types of media?

---

advertisement notice that calls attention to a product or an event

New media

Computers are all around us. Since the 1990s, computers and digital media have become the most popular ways for people to get their news and entertainment.

People today can read books, magazines and newspapers using their mobile phones and the internet. TVs are digital too. People can listen to music, stream films and play video games on their TVs. People even create their own media using digital media. Online blogs, photo books and stop-motion films are examples of digital media.

FACT! There are more mobile phones in the world today than people.

Making media

Media tells or shows us a message using words, pictures and sound. We read, listen to and watch media everywhere we go. We also write and draw media to share messages and ideas. With a computer, tablet or smartphone, anyone can create media. Today there are **apps** people use to make videos and record music.

---

app programme that is downloaded to computers and mobile devices; app is short for application

Try it!

Get ready to make your own media! Tell a story by making your own film or comic strip. First, think of a short story. Draw three pictures to tell the beginning, middle and end.

If you can, use a tablet or mobile phone to take photos of the three pictures. Ask an adult to help you find a film-making app. Next, follow the instructions to add sound or your voice to the pictures. Then, share your film or comic strip with your friends and family.

Think about it!

How many examples of media can you find right now? What types of media can you see?

21

Glossary

advertisement notice that calls attention to a product or an event

app programme that is downloaded to computers and mobile devices; app is short for application

audience people who hear, read or see a message

billboard large outdoor sign used to advertise products or services

broadcast TV or radio programme

logo symbol of a company's brand

quality standard of something as measured against other things of a similar type

recorded written or filmed so that it can be used or seen again in the future

Books

I Can Write Stories (I Can Write), Anita Ganeri (Raintree, 2013)

Let's Think About the Internet and Social Media (Let's Think About), Alex Woolf (Raintree, 2015)

Using Digital Technology (Our Digital Planet), Ben Hubbard (Raintree, 2017)

Websites

www.bbc.co.uk/newsround
The BBC newsround website is an example of online media, where you can explore news events and play games and quizzes.

www.dkfindout.com/uk/more-find-out/special-events/how-is-book-made/
Find out more about print media by learning how a book is made.

Comprehension questions

1. Describe three types of media.

2. What are the three main reasons we use media?

3. What is the purpose of advertising?

Index